anythin'

First Facts

ANCIENT EGYPT

GODS AND GODDESSES OF ANCIENT EGYPT

JANEEN R. ADIL

Consultant:
Leo Depuydt
Professor, Department of Egyptology and
Ancient Western Asian Studies
Brown University
Providence, Rhode Island

Capstone press

Mankato, Minnesota

First Facts are published by Capstone Press,
151 Good Counsel Drive, P.O. Box 669, Mankato, Minnesota 56002.
www.capstonepress.com

Library of Congress Cataloging-in-Publication Data
Adil, Janeen R.
    Gods and goddesses of ancient Egypt / by Janeen R. Adil.
    p. cm. — (First facts. Ancient Egypt)
    Includes bibliographical references and index.
    Summary: "Describes some of the main gods and goddesses of ancient Egypt, including how they looked, the
role they played in Egyptian life, and how they were worshipped" — Provided by publisher.
    ISBN-13: 978-1-4296-1991-2 (hardcover)
    ISBN-10: 1-4296-1991-0 (hardcover)
    1. Gods, Egyptian — Juvenile literature. 2. Goddesses, Egyptian — Juvenile literature. 3. Mythology,
Egyptian — Juvenile literature. I. Title. II. Series.
BL2441.3.A35 2009
299'.31211 — dc22   2008000274

Editorial Credits
Christine Peterson, editor; Alison Thiele, designer; Wanda Winch, photo researcher; Marcy Morin, page 21,
    project production

Photo Credits
Alamy/Ancient Art and Architecture, 11; Alamy/Andrew Holt, 7 (top right); Alamy/Mary Evans Picture
Library, 12–13; Alamy/Robert Harding Picture Library Ltd., 16; Alamy/TRIP, 15 (left); Art Life Images/Sylvain
Grandadam, 7 (left); Art Resource, N.Y./ Giraudon, 17; Art Resource, N.Y./Réunion des Musées Nationaux,
19; Capstone Press/Karon Dubke, 21; Landov LLC/Reuters/Aladin Abdel Naby, 18; Photri-MicroStock, 15
(top right); Shutterstock/Elnur, 5; Shutterstock/Marek Szumlas, cover; Shutterstock/Mirek Hejnicki, 20;
Shutterstock/Steve Dern, 8; Shutterstock/Tatiana Grozetskaya, 1; Shutterstock/YKh, (background throughout)

Essential content terms are bold and are defined at the bottom of the page where they first appear.

072010
5843VMI

TABLE OF CONTENTS

ANCIENT BELIEFS

The ancient Egyptians built a strong and rich country. They gave thanks to gods and goddesses for these good things. Egyptians **worshipped** thousands of gods and goddesses. To honor them, Egyptians built huge stone temples and statues. Temples were homes for gods and goddesses.

worship: to show great honor

ANCIENT EGYPT

The time in history called ancient Egypt began around 3000 BC, about 5,000 years ago. It ended in 30 BC, when Rome took over Egypt.

Inside each temple was a statue of a god. Priests bathed the statue and offered it food.

WORSHIPPING GODS AND GODDESSES

Egyptians worshipped their gods and goddesses in different ways. Only **pharaohs** and priests could worship in temples. Most Egyptians prayed to gods and goddesses at home. Some people visited public **shrines** to worship and give thanks.

pharaoh: an Egyptian king
shrine: a place where people worship

Statue of Ramses II

Ancient Egyptian temple

HIDDEN STATUE

The town of Abydos was associated with the god Osiris. It was an important religious center. Ancient Egyptians met there to worship. Scientists later dug up the area. They found a statue of pharaoh Ramses II. The king was dressed like Osiris to honor the god.

7

RE, THE SUN GOD

Re (or Ra) was the sun god. He had a man's body with a falcon's head. Egyptians believed Re created the world. Each day, he would travel across the sky in a sun boat.

Egyptians also believed Re was the father of their kings. A pharaoh would call himself "The Son of Re."

DISCOVER!

Pharaohs were the link between the gods and the people. Egyptians believed their kings became gods after death.

ISIS, THE HEALER

Isis was one of Egypt's earliest and most beloved goddesses. Isis had magical powers and protected the Egyptians. She was also a healer. Isis was shown as a queen. On her head, Isis wore the sign for "throne."

DISCOVER!

Egyptians believed a star called Sirius represented Isis. The appearance of this star marked the beginning of a New Year.

11

Osiris

UNDERWORLD GODS

Osiris was god of the **Underworld**. He judged the dead. Osiris had the form of a **mummy**. He sometimes wore a white crown with two feathers. In his hands he often carried a ruler's whip and curved cane.

mummy: a body that has been preserved

Underworld: a place where Egyptians believed spirits went

Anubis

Anubis was a god of **embalming**. He was shown as a dog or a man with a dog's head. He guided the dead to the Underworld. He weighed their hearts to see if they had led a good life.

embalming: a way to preserve a dead body

13

NEITH, GODDESS OF WAR

Neith was goddess of war and hunting. On her head was a red crown. She carried a shield and two arrows that crossed.

Neith also protected people who wove cloth. The **linen** used to wrap a mummy was said to be her gift.

linen: a cloth made from the flax plant

DISCOVER!

Egyptians believed Neith settled disputes between other gods.

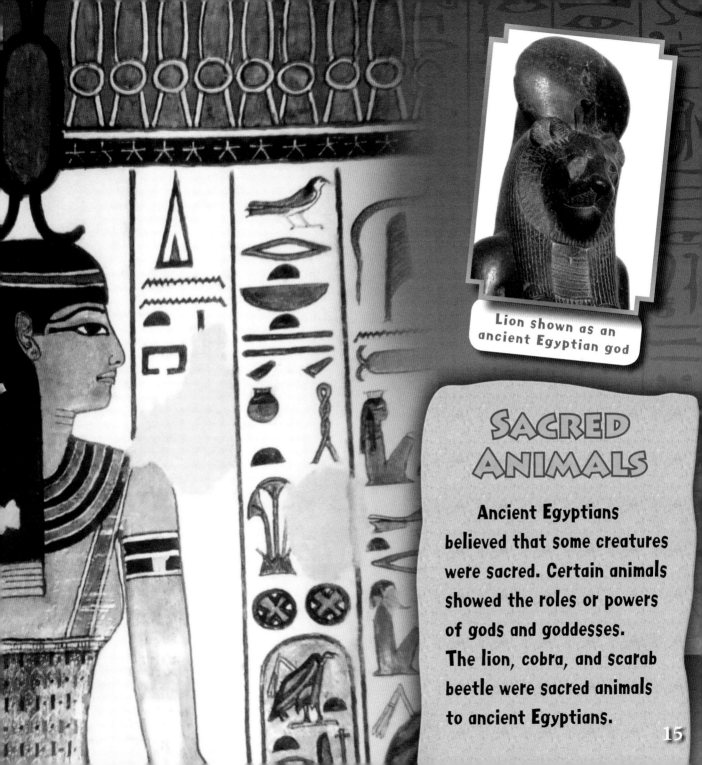

Lion shown as an ancient Egyptian god

SACRED ANIMALS

Ancient Egyptians believed that some creatures were sacred. Certain animals showed the roles or powers of gods and goddesses. The lion, cobra, and scarab beetle were sacred animals to ancient Egyptians.

CREATOR AND SKY GODS

Amun was an early creator god. He wore a crown with two tall feathers. Amun was often combined with the sun god, Re. Then he was a more powerful god called Amun-Re.

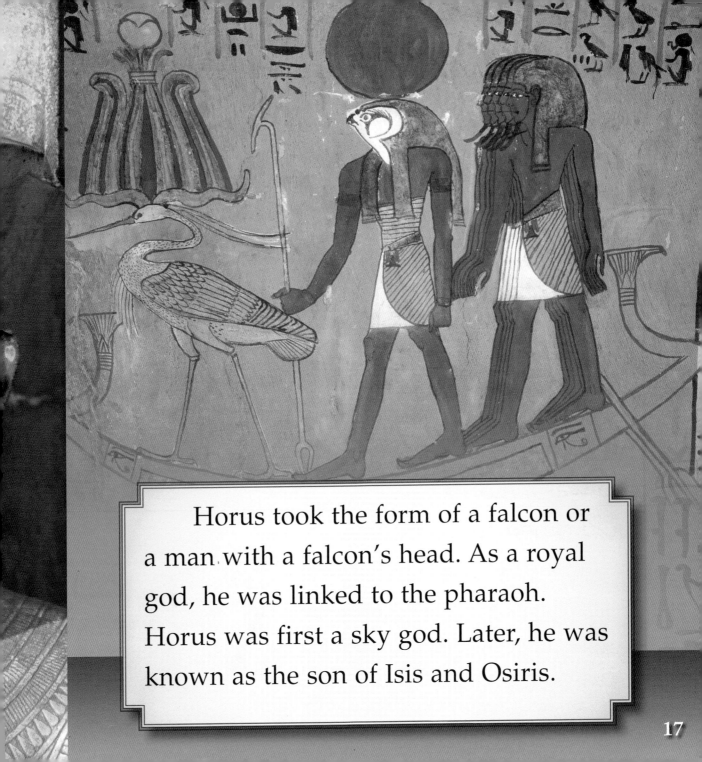

Horus took the form of a falcon or a man with a falcon's head. As a royal god, he was linked to the pharaoh. Horus was first a sky god. Later, he was known as the son of Isis and Osiris.

HAPPINESS, LOVE, AND BEAUTY

Bastet was a goddess of happiness. She took the form of a cat or woman with a cat's head. Because of her, Egyptians treated cats with respect.

Hathor was goddess of music, dance, love, and beauty. Egyptians believed she was their pharaohs' mother. Hathor often wore a crown shaped like a sun disk with horns.

In the 1960s, Egyptians built a dam across the Nile River. The dam caused water to flood a temple honoring Isis. The temple had to be taken apart and moved. The pieces were placed on higher ground. Like a puzzle, about 40,000 stone blocks were put back together. In 1980, the temple was completed.

Philae temple honoring Isis

HANDS ON: A CAT MASK

Ancient Egyptians kept cats as pets. These animals were also sacred to the goddess Bastet. The Egyptians created many beautiful statues of cats. Make your own Egyptian cat mask complete with royal jewelry.

What You Need

- paper plate
- black paint
- paintbrush
- scissors
- black construction paper
- glue
- white or gold paint
- black pipe cleaners
- craft stick
- colored beads

What You Do

1. Paint the paper plate black.

2. Cut out triangles from the black paper. These will be the cat's ears. Glue them to the back of the paper plate.

3. Use the white or gold paint to add eyes in the Egyptian style. Use black paint to line the eyes. You can also paint a mouth and nose.

4. Using glue, add pipe cleaners for whiskers and the craft stick for a handle. Glue on beads to make a necklace for your cat.

Glossary

embalming (im-BALM-ing) — preserving a dead body so it does not decay

linen (LIN-uhn) — a cloth made from the flax plant

mummy (MUH-mee) — a body that has been preserved with special salts and cloth

pharaoh (FAIR-oh) — a king of ancient Egypt

shrine (SHRINE) — a holy building

Underworld (UHN-dur-wurld) — the place under the earth where ancient Egyptians believed spirits of the dead go

worship (WUR-ship) — to express love or honor to a higher being

READ MORE

Benduhn, Tea. *Ancient Egypt*. Life Long Ago. Milwaukee: Weekly Reader Early Learning Library, 2007.

Ferris, Julie. *Life and Times in Ancient Egypt*. Boston: Kingfisher, 2007.

Ganeri, Anita. *Ancient Egyptians*. Ancient Civilizations. Minneapolis: Compass Point Books, 2007.

INTERNET SITES

FactHound offers a safe, fun way to find Internet sites related to this book. All of the sites on FactHound have been researched by our staff.

Here's how:
1. Visit *www.facthound.com*
2. Choose your grade level.
3. Type in this book ID **1429619910** for age-appropriate sites. You may also browse subjects by clicking on letters, or by clicking on pictures and words.
4. Click on the **Fetch It** button.

FactHound will fetch the best sites for you!

INDEX